TURNING THE KEY

Also by Lotte Kramer

Ice-Break (Annakinn, 1980)
Family Arrivals (Poet & Printer, 1981 & 1992)
A Lifelong House (Hippopotamus Press, 1983)
The Shoemaker's Wife (Hippopotamus Press, 1987)
The Desecration of Trees (Hippopotamus Press, 1994)
Earthquake & Other Poems (Rockingham Press, 1994)
Selected & New Poems 1980-1997 (Rockingham Press, 1997)
Heimweh-Homesick, ed. Beate Hörr (Brandes & Apsel, 1999)
The Phantom Lane (Rockingham Press, 2000)
Black Over Red (Rockingham Press, 2005)
Kindertransport, Before & After: Elegy & Celebration,
ed. Sybil Oldfield (University of Sussex, 2007)
A Selection published in Japan, ed. & trans. Junko Kimura
(Sapporo, 2007)

Lotte Kramer

Turning the Key

Rockingham Press

Published in 2009 by
The Rockingham Press
11 Musley Lane,
Ware, Herts SG12 7EN
www.rockinghampress.com

British Library Cataloguing-in-Publication Data

A catalogue record for this book
is available from the British Library

ISBN 978-1-904851-30-1

Printed in Great Britain
by the MPG Books Group

FOR FREDDIE

'But who would count eternity in days?
These old bones live to learn her wanton ways:
 (I measure time by how the body sways).'

                    Theodore Roethke   (*I Knew a Woman*)

'I have asked for my childhood
and it has returned and I feel
that it is still as hard as at that time,
and that it has been no use
getting older.'

                    Extract from *Malte Laurids Brigge*
                              Rainer Maria Rilke

Contents

ENGADINE POEMS – a sequence

VERSIONS AND TRANSLATIONS

Acknowledgements

With thanks to the editors of magazines where some of these poems first appeared:

Acumen, Agenda, Ambit, Artemis, Candelabrum, European Judaism, Interpreter's House, Jewish Renaissance, Kindertransport (University of Sussex), *Lapis Lazuli, The London Magazine, New Headland, Other Poetry, Poetry Review, Poetry Canada Review, Quattrocento, The Rialto, Scintilla, Second Light Newsletter, Urthona, Ver Poets' Anthology* and *Warwick Review.*

Identity

A river, wandering
Through a bed of rocks
Never quite
Homing in one place,
Tasting the difference
Of earth's
Textures, lushness
And dryness for my
Long journey,
A constant movement,
Exploring this gift
But also
A losing on foreign shores
Where languages jar
On my waters'
Fluidity, preventing
Arrival at the sea's throat.
A stagnant
Sojourn of black
Solitude, a stage of scorn
At liquid living
Of inevitable yearning
And slow acceptance,
A song
Of searching voices
For the many and the one.

Books

Today the books are my sole companions
They all want their faces, wiped, their spines
Dusted, their habitats on shelves assured
Whatever their personalities

Or stories might be. They want me to save
Them, to remember their origins
To preserve their languages even if enslaved
In the past, with outdated histories.

But I have a soft spot for them all.
They tell me who I am and who I was.
Even if shelf space is running out, they call
To me not to abandon them, not lose

Their many voices in the turmoil bred
In our loud-mouthed computer world.

A Dream

You were a child again,
An eight-year old, a cub,
And had to leave our home.
I walked along with you
Where viaducts and squares
Exchanged each other, where
The roads were peopled, cluttered
In an unknown city.
And all the way your chat
Was trust, assuring me
That you'd be happy where
You'll have to be alone.
Some flats confronted us,
The continental type,
The sunset pockmarked their grey
Stone. 'Up there,' you said
And pointed to the third
Etage, 'that's where the people
Live who'll take me in.'
And then I knew I'd lost –
You were so keen to go.

My way home was confused.
Some endless streets and stairs
That led to marble windows,
Hidden doors, some churches
Tall and derelict with workmen
Pinned like brooches to their sides,
Painting, restoring.
They pointed to my left:
A sudden harbour opened up
To ocean-going ships
In silent, widening space.
Alone I felt at peace.

East Wind

When the East wind
Crossed the Rhine from Siberia
Cutting into bodies and faces

Piercing the double windows
So that felt curtains flapped
Even in a heated room,

I walked with my mother
Up the hill to our house
Staying well behind her

Burying my face in her back,
Her fur-coat a protection,
A warm hairiness

In semi-darkness all the way
With the wind whistling round us
Propelling us forward.

I was about half her height
But can feel it still now:
This fur-faced walking uphill.

Note: my thanks to Jane Duran for the trigger.

Rhine

Always the father of my being
Unchanging in your majestic song.

My earliest memory, a child's wonder,
There beside you on the sandy shore

Watching the flow of your silver streaming
Taking barges with coal and clothing

All through Europe, gipsies of water,
The flags of countries' colours flutter.

You witness borders, wars and vineyards
Pleasure steamers with singing bards,

Slimy steps took me down to your coolness
Learning to swim in your sheltering fastness.

History lives in your towns and villages
Blasting through Roman and baroque treasures,

Crusaders rampaged through Jewish Quarters,
Still you protect with assuring presence.

Needlework

She taught me needlework
With gentleness.
A big, kind woman
In her twenties still
With repetitive and a sleepy voice.

"You thread the needle and
  You pull it through,
  Ruck-zuck with regularity,
  To get the even-measured stitches
  In your work, continuously."

Cruel we were, sneering
At her monotony
So many years ago,
Allowing now a sudden memory
To face her disappearance then.

Recorder

In a drawer it rests
Now unplayed,
Chestnut-grained wood;
Many years ago
In another life,
My first musical
Instrument
Evoking a simple tune
With lizard fingers,
The music teacher's
Patient imprint
On my receptive self,
Leading to the more ample
Sound of the piano.
Yet persisting in the lone
Flute-like lament,
Silently unheard
For her whose life
Was shattered.

Note: her career as a musicologist was ended by Nazi race laws. She committed suicide.

First Channel Crossing

It was as if
   The grey sky filled the ground
      Rolling its edgeless dawn
         Into an open cloud.

We left a house,
   The continents of night
      And day; on roads, in trains;
         And fourteen early years
            In fisted streets, where eyes
               And footsteps haunted stones.

Now that first sight
   Of sea was endlessness:
      Convoking rings of shade
         And newness in this mist.

Amoeba

     Always
The taste of shipwreck
   On my tongue;
   Salty
And rusty as
   The scabrous sea
   Whose weight
Of water strangles,
   Calcifies.
   And yet
That icy knowledge
   Alters me:
   I touch
Its sign, I swim
   My other life.

Ode to M.F.
Who met our Kindertransport

She met us in a grim-grey station
And warmth spilled from her eyes,
A light on that smoked-filled morning
Surrounded and spread from her side.

Her Irish voice was melodious,
Her exuberance infected us all,
She could love and hate profoundly
And her temperament held us in thrall.

There was space for us in her house,
Quite bohemian in every way,
And she cooked huge meals on her kitchen range
In a slap-dash manner each day.

We all flocked to her for protections,
Refugees from life and war,
And her Schubert songs and her Dickens
Filled our evenings by the fire.

So this ode to her and her memory
For the life of art she shared
With a generous heart and gesture
That lives on and defies the world.

1939

Then, to improve my English,
I learnt some poetry by heart.
I loved the Shakespeare sonnets:
"When in disgrace with fortune
  And men's eyes I all alone beweep ..."
I quoted it to the cleaning lady
Who looked at me in bafflement,
Had no idea what I meant.
In time I realized that language
Is in flux, has changed its music.
My love stayed undiminished.

A Foiled Arrest

"They came to arrest us, English police,
My father, brother and myself, the war
In early stages still. They had to seize
Suspicious enemy aliens, so we were

Categorised. They did not realize
Our loyalty was not to the Nazi state,
Germany, the country of our birth but
England, now our home and refuge place.

I had just left to do my war-work in
A factory as engineer, my father
Was an old man, at home, a former lawyer,
Unemployed, my soldier-brother sleeping

Off Dunkirk came down in uniform –
They left, apologised, did not return."

The Sleeping Bow-tie

A crocheted bow-tie
Sleeps in my chest of drawers.

My mother made it
In quiet days.

It has never been worn,
A useless piece

And yet I cannot
Discard it.

Sleep on, sleep on,
Join her ashes

From a long way off
Together with mine.

My Father's Writing

My father's writing was a work of art.
His spidery letters of the German
Alphabet danced in a filigree that
Veiled and spiked the page in one great span

With Gothic structures in their evenness
And elegance. You could decipher how
He built and shaped his life's experiences
Into his words and sentences to show

The solitary schoolboy walking miles
To town, the witty playwright with his cast,
The wounded soldier with his wartime mates,
Then braving worlds of finance, civvy-street.

Throughout his style remained impeccable
Yet something in himself stayed unfulfilled.

Jam

That red sweet-sour caress
On the tongue
Delight of summer fruits
We take for granted,
A sudden reminder
Of that starving man *
In his confined, shared
Lodging house
Some sixty years ago
Stealing in passing
The occasional spoonful
Of another inmate's jam.

* *Viktor Klemperer*

Boomerang

You
Who desecrate the dead
With venom
Coating your hands
Daubing
That crooked cross
On sacred stones
Leaving
Them broken to the open sky –
Hatred
Will boomerang and burn
Your hearts.

For a Released Hostage

Behind his eyes
Are chains and darkened rooms,
Behind his smile
A cubicle of fear,
The years of hunger lurk
Behind his youth
And lasso shadows
Stumbling on his path.

A tree: "A miracle"
Will save him still,
Lessen his nightmares
And the claws of time.

The Victims
(Tsunami)

Their sea and wind-blown lives
Escape to nothingness,
Anchor in
A giant's mouth
For ever.

The Bus Driver
7.07.05

He turned and saw his bus was cut in half,
Quite dazed and shattered he climbed from his seat
And started walking from the wreck, the carved-up
Vehicle; the mutilated left

Behind, the blood, the screaming bodies
In the street. So he walked west and west again
Into a blindness, part of his release
In terror-trance, just pavements leading him

Further away. He, unaware of spattered
Blood spotting his uniform, his leaden face.
And still he walked like someone fettered
To a horse taking him from this maze.

For seven miles his legs performed this ritual
To land inside a suburb's hospital.

Turning the Key

I shut the door on him
And turn the key
To leave him in his solitary cell.

The night-time prison sinks
Into his grey abyss
With only shrieks that surface from the dark.

Some knocking will grow weaker
As the hours pass,
Some nightmares throttle fragmentary sleep.

I fight against the horror
Of the ghostly key
Shutting the door on my own loneliness.

Saltness

As we leave the marshes
The gulls have the last word,
Their fierce cry echoes the wind
That pin-points this coastline.

The mud is the colour of iron
Coating exuberant children
As they slide into the cut
Empty now of sea water.

It has been a new holiday
Experience, not our favourite
Landscape, in utter contrast
To mountains. We are learning

To salute the sea's saltness.

Stone

Whenever I think of red sandstone
I see the Rhineland cathedrals,
The churches with their soft baroque,
Their graceful angles and steeples,
Some perched on hillsides,
Some in the centre of cities,
Islands of crumbling peace
With incense snaking through cracks
Intoxicating and soothing
Even for unbelievers like us.
In contrast, the hard granite
Found in mountains, high up,
Veined with history and iron,
Mementos on a kitchen sill.

Haiku

I am a stranger
To the words of the sea, a
Land and tree lover

Perspective

'It were an old-fashioned summer,' he said
Straightening up from the lawn,
'And the winter before no winter at all.'
Too true, I nodded my head.
'Old-fashioned' I thought,
Like walking to school
When the heat was beating down
Along dusty streets, on cobblestones,
With my satchel weighing a ton,
And between the stones
There, the black tar
Was oozing in the sun
As black as a beetle
But soft as cream –
I can feel it now:
That plasticine touch
As I scraped it
And moulded it in my palm,
Yielding astonishment.

Stationary

Warm and soft
The colour grey
Covers our days.
Depressing for some
But I say I like
That undemanding evenness,
The background
To the mundane
Time of the year
When sleep has
Invaded gardens,
Wind hardly stirs
The few redundant
Leaves. The man
Opposite busies
Himself with cutting
Stationary grass.

A Wounded Nerve

"I sold a picture last week."
He stirs his coffee slowly.
Our painter-window-cleaner
Sits in my kitchen sadly.

"I studied History and Art,
 Tried teaching, could not stand it,
 The strain, the concentration
 Was too much. A break-down then."

A gentle, tall, good-looking
Man, smartly turned-out.
Got married once, produced
A child, but now alone.

"Marriage was not for me."
His paintings tell of landscapes
In their truth and birth,
His colours shine a wounded nerve.

Out windows gleam their clarity.

Unicycle Rider

(Ernst Ludwig Kirchner)

1.
In this jungle forest
I stick to the path
On my unicycle
Not expecting
To meet a soul
Until suddenly
You appear
Walking towards me.
Was I glad?
Halfway yes
Though I might have seen
My own reflection
Had I been alone,
Had a new experience,
An exploration
Of my unknown self.
Instead I touched your head,
My possession,
Your familiarity
Reassuring yet
What have I missed?

2.
You flatter yourself.
I was walking for my own sake,
To breathe the air
Of unencumbered loneliness.
To find the freedom
Among trees and bushes
Away from the mechanics
Of streets and houses.
But your touch
Has made me lame,
Put a halt
To suspected otherness.

The Portuguese Jewish Cemetery, 1655
(Jacob van Ruisdael)

A blighted tree
A sentry guards this place
While water trickles over rocks
Into a brook.

The stones are scattered
Among shrubs and grasses,
Haphazard almost, white and black,
They've lost their way.

Some rabbis buried with their books
Where Hebrew script had surfaced
On the earth for talk to passers-by,
Now perished, gone.

Some upturned roots,
Some ruined arches, columns
Frame the backdrop adding mystery,
A mass of trees.

And furious clouds
Explode from ink to blue
To strident white above the site
In a Vesuvian shout.

Stillness
(Vilhelm Hammershøi)

From the back
The young woman resting,
Tenderness of the bone in her neck.

A pattern of sunlight
Through window panes
Marking the floor's bareness

Illuminating squares
Of transparencies
To a game of hopscotch.

On the polished table
A cup, untouched
In powdery light, in silence.

Door gleaming white
Open on to other doors,
Corridors enclosed, empty.

Everywhere emptiness,
Only dust motes dancing
On a sunbeam, slanting.

And the woman in black
A column standing
In stillness and peace.

An Old Woman Cooking Eggs
(Velazquez)

With wisdom she cradles the egg in her hand
And answers the questioning boy while her spoon
Is poised over sizzling eggs in the pot.
All is simple, the red terracotta is hot,
The knife is laid on the edge of the dish.
With her handsome old face she turns to the boy
Confirming her grandmother's hidden bond.

Mascot in a Museum

He sits upright in a glass case
Surveying his new surroundings.

The years have greyed his white fur
To a threadbare blotchy coat

And hands that used to hold him
Are only a distant memory

And yet they survive in this small shape
That failed to save the young

Engineer from the icy waters
Swallowing his crew as well.

Note: A small Steiff bear, mascot of an engineer on the 'Titanic', William Young Moyes.

Aphrodite, Rhodes Museum

Out of dry earth she came
    Perfect in her repose.
He, who had shaped her then
    Must have known light on stone
Could so retrieve warm flesh,
    Must have seen arms design
Angles to hair and head,
    Watched how the waist could curve
Finding a shadow there,
    Smooth at the thigh's escape,
Touching a whiteness where
    Marble and earth must meet.

There, by the water's edge,
    Kneeling she turned to ask
Him who had carved her so
    Never to love new flesh.

Three Returns

Reading of love,
Their lifelong universe,
I shut the book.
Eyes blind with ache and tense
With hoarded rust.
I know one gesture tells
Of years, one look
Can summon light and fears
Will fall to dust.
Return brings homeless dark.

At Passover
They gravely pray for Zion.
A coming home.
I stood there, saw them sway
In that rose-glove
Of stone. Jerusalem
Was not my soil.
Only Lot's wife remains,
Hard in her blood,
Her turning struck to salt,
Her longing cold.

I think of one grooved face,
Low-ringed by light;
She held her glass of gin
Tight in thin hands
And talked of love: 'You think
    You've planed the height
    Only to meet its groan
    Years cannot mend.'
And as we left the inn
Each turned to find
Another table laid.

In Rome

Prayers, like sea-spray,
From the stones of Rome,
Older than fountains
Washing stillness.

In volcanic earth,
Between columns,
Under jewelled domes,
The supplications

Move with skeletons
Of years, their bones
Are dense with noise
Of all humanity.

Apart, in the dark rooms
Of Keats, with hope
As eloquent as the rain
On his sheltered grave,

I believe in the coinage
Of words as ancient
As the pushing
March crowds outside.

The Ampersand

You face me
Like an autumn leaf
Hungry for familiar branches,

We eat together
And slowly you find
Your way to our tree,

The knowledge:
A terrifying gift
We untie only at intervals,

The ampersand:
A touch on the knot
Of the invisible chord.

The Necklace

That time on holiday in Switzerland
You did surprise me with a necklace I'd
Admired, standing outside a jeweller's
Shop, a modest one with pearls, grey-toned.

I treasured it, not prone to ornaments.
It was the simple beauty of design
That spoke to me, the thinness of the chain,
The tiny pearls like petit-pois that lent

A warmth to this so unexpected gift.
It meant Saas-Fee, the tallest mountain Dôme
Daring us up into the glacier's climb,
Into the fear that comes with air and height.

I lost it. Still a journey's mystery loot,
More than a blessing round my ageing throat.

Rain

After too many voices
The soft rain coated our walk.

Distances were carefully
Reassembled over the hills.

Then we paused in her who loved
This unhurried rain; who used
To tear off her scarf,

Open her coat and hair
Offering face and neck
To its cool rhythm.

In her the elements rejoiced
And suffered. In her we cross

The alternate answer –
In discord and stillness of clouds.

This Falling Fear

The shortest day:
Slowly, the bruised light fails,
A gentle fear;

Not like that time
When all I saw was white
Aggression, glare:

The nurse's dress.
It hurt my eyes after
Their nine years' dark.

I had to learn
To understand a face
Behind the voice.

Even my mother's.
Not use my hands as eyes
Feeling the warmth

Of dogs and cats,
But look astonished at
The living sky,

See parables
Of colours everywhere:
This woman's hand,

That swollen rain
Repeating all the shades
Of earth and leaves

Or someone's hair –
And now this falling fear:
Tomorrow's day!

Facts

"My spine has gone"
She heaved herself out of a chair
And plunged into the kitchen
Making tea – would not
Accept my help.
Then laser-beamed
Across the room at me,
Her gleaming house a document,
Her home-made bread and biscuits
Victory.
A shelf of jams,
A line of books,
A wheelchair
In the hall.

On Age

I watch him stumble, falter, hold my breath,
Not show him the anxiety I feel,
Not sap his confidence, not make him fail
In his mobility, a living death.

That age should come to this is cruelty,
Attack his walker's knees with seering pain,
Stiffen his joints, his ankles, let him claim
His former hiker's self as parody.

No compensation can affirm enough
The loss of years and youth that takes its toll
On those of us confronting living rough
Old age and looking back on to a full

And active earlier time. We have to try
And find the beauty hidden in each day.

Fear

Like the end of a bright passage
Extinguishing light
There looms in utter silence
The bereavement of words.
The absence of images threatens
Into dawn-grey void
Where every thought is unworthy
Of the alphabet, the sentence.
Where even memory
With its summits and its Hades
Remains an untouchable act,
A mourned-for spring, now dry.
Even an ancestor's face
Is a parchment never-land
Refusing to be explored.
The sacredness of trees and rivers,
Of mountains in their mysteries
Demanding prayer of worship
Will go unanswered.

Search

I am looking for a beautiful line
To lift me high from the daily routine.

They used to come to meet me before
But lately they will retreat to a shore

Of forgetfulness and unknowing
Where they hide and grow strange voices,

Not in my vocabulary. A darkness
Nails them to the other side of gladness.

A Walk Across Centuries

Not an indifferent ball-pen
But a small black fountain-pen
Still from childhood years
Full of shiny character.

It needs refilling too often,
Runs out in mid-sentence
Like someone with loss of memory
Hungry for indelible black ink.

I treasure it, use it every day,
Sign my books with its
Broad golden nib,
An intimate bridge between us.

A walk across centuries.
I love to hold it, handle it
Though it smudges the fingers
Of my arthritic hands.

Later

Later – the word is surrounded
By a mist of grey vagueness,
Possibilities colour it syllables
Lighting a flame of reward,
Of hopefulness for future living.
A promise in the slow scale
Of its music drawn out in the first
Vowel but dissolving – later,
Like this rain a constant companion
Initialling a pre-spring day.

The Insect

The years have stolen sound.
I cannot hear my footsteps any more,
I mourn the loss of drowned

High notes, the voices in a song.
The radio will not compromise
Nor will the telephone.

The insect in my ear
Is alien to my skin and bones,
It does not pacify, it is not true.

Two Crows

Two crows
On top of a bare winter tree
Huge and black
They fly into space and return
Again and again
For what?

Flower

Flower
Closing your petals at night
Your porcelain face
A shut question mark
You will open it
In daylight as answer
To my searching.

Nameless

Wildflowers,
I don't even know their names
But they stand up to my waist
Near the river's laziness,
Their scentless
Colours pinned into grasses
Where water's peculiar smell
Rises like fermenting yeast.
Solitude,
How I love your quiet summer
Away from well-polished lawns;
This voicelessly brushing breeze
Healing through
Fleshy and feathery blades
Lending a name to my own
Transparent winter retreat.

Escaping Worship

From my window
The mountains zig-zag
To their peaks
Inviting a line
Of escaping worship.
Below we step
On thyme-scented grass.

Lament for Autumn

Now autumn buries autumn
    And the ground
Is premature with sleep.

The half-light spends itself
    In moody days
That seem afraid to wake entirely;

And where the rust burnt noisily
    In that last leaf,
A charcoal branch mourns in the wind.

And we, who want escape from pain
    But harbour
Greater fear of dull complacency,

Must summon all the patience
    Of the hidden light
And so reflect the year.

Forest Evenings

Spun out like skeins of wool
These summer evenings. Smells
Heighten their acuteness, pine

Penetrates the obesity of day.
All is clarity – the dog's bark,
The boy's ball bouncing:

A thunderclap through still air.
Clumps of harebells more blue
Than at any other time.

Outline of trees as clear-cut
As lace edges against the sky.
Cruelty at its most improbable.

Rilke

'Schoengeistigkeit' so spurned the veteran's word.
But you, under so many lids asleep,
Are fire-tongued with scalpel and white petal
That must replace our wilful ugliness.

No consciousness can celebrate enough
The angel's oldest order and his terror;
Nor shape in reason – from a fragrance – life
To equal your concise and utter birth.

Dream Train

This train never stops.
I'm a parcelled person
In its warm movement,
Assured of eventual stations.

No decisions required.
No steps can be taken,
Passive yet static,
The ritual vibrations.

Voices surround me
Without new hearing.
Waiting means sureness
Of compound travelling.

ENGADINE POEMS
a sequence

The Same World

An earth-tremor inland
We knew nothing of
While walking over roots,
Under rain-sharpened trees
On stony soil
Not far away
The wounded earth
Shook in agony.

So it was then,
When breath was choked
Out of their bodies
Under a hostile sky
And we danced
The 'Lambeth Walk'
On another continent
In the same world.

Cameo

Outside the café
A bearded student
Plays Bach on his violin.
Occasional coins tumble
Rarely into a box.
Uncertain weather
Makes people moody,
Has put cloud-weights
On holiday spirit.
Yet the morning soared
Blue and white over peaks
With silent generosity,
Have they forgotten so soon?

Private

"Piz Languard, Muattas Muragl"
Such solid round names
Strewn here like large harebells;
Not yet Italian but Romansch,
The private language of the Engadin.
I could listen to that Glockenspiel-sound
For hours. Today we were lifted up
To the alp in those dizzy chairs,
Almost brushing tree-tops, rocks;
We are air – so much air and sky
With peaks all around! I'm a pinhead!

Morteratsch Approach

From troll-country and forest
We are approaching the giant glacier:
A congregation of stones and rocks,
White-grey, pays homage with us
Till we stand staring at his huge
Stepping ice face.
Water forms in small falls
Or trickles underfoot baptising
The river from his many orifices.

Nothing gentle here. Only
Grasses and heathers braving wind.
We dwindle with all other creatures
To coloured earth-dots strewn on boulders.
Yet we read every few yards
About his shrinking and retreat:
The glacier withdrawing year by year
With willpower we cannot enter.

ENGADINE POEMS

Fex Valley

It draws and rings us in,
This valley with its river pulse
Beating a centre tune

Through leaning walls of meadows.
Cowbells chime their fat bequest
Generous as uncles.

Snow peaks attack to lend their light
To forest mystery
Asserting their cold element.

We wander through a rainbow sea
Of wild flowers pushing
And bending their mastery

Over seasons. Accepting
The ballet of change
They dance their summer song

As wind controls the leash.
We turn reluctantly
Losing each step in its mesh.

Triolet

The scarlet train unwinds itself
In spirals to the village church.
With every octave down the shelf
The scarlet train unwinds itself
Soprano tree-tops rise, the gulf
Our dolls' eyes see will shrink and lurch.
The scarlet train unwinds itself
In spirals to the village church.

Premature

Our skin still brown from yesterday's sun
Today we flee under a sky
Littered with snow flakes, we run

To take shelter and find a dry
Doorway to look at Christmas trees
That have supplanted butterflies

And insects. The mountains
Have vanished, instead a thick fleece
Of grey wool covers all heights.

The seasons have changed over night
Leaping across autumn
In one gigantic sprint

But it is premature, too soon
We know the sun is lying in wait
And will demolish that white sin

In an hour, and look, by late
Afternoon the valley is green again,
Flowers resurrect themselves in light,

The Swiss flag too, on the roof garden,
Turns its full red-cross face to me,
Has found a new direction.

ENGADINE POEMS

Idyll

We sit at the feet
Of snow-lit mountains
And stare at their white

Their glacial bleakness
Softened by sunlight,
A puncture in blueness.

Beside us a house
By the edge of a wood
In a dell of long grass,

A smoking chimney,
A barking dog,
A porch of blond timber.

Above a lake
Like a lone dwarf
At peace for its sake.

VERSIONS AND TRANSLATIONS

The Loneliest One (fragment)
after Friedrich Nietzsche

Now, that the day
Was tired of the day, and all the longing brooks
Are splashing with new consolation,
And all the heavens hung with golden cobwebs
Are telling every tired one: "Rest now!" –
Why don't you rest, you darkest heart,
What stings you into footsore flight …
Whom are you hoping for?

Brevity
(Friedrich Hölderlin)

"Why are you so brief? Don't you love song any more
  As you did before? A young man in days of hope
  You sang without ever
  Finding an end to it."

My song is like my happiness. – Do you want to bathe
  Joyfully in sunset light? It has gone and earth is cold,
  And the night bird is whirring
  Uncomfortably in front of your eye.

The Half of Life
(Friedrich Hölderlin)

With yellow pears
And full of wild roses
The land hangs into the lake,
You gracious swans
Drunk with kissing
You dip your heads
Into holy-sobering water.

Woe me, where shall I take
The flowers from in winter,
And where the sunshine,
And shadows of earth?
The walls are standing
Speechless and cold, the flags
Jangle in the wind.

Abisag

after Rainer Maria Rilke

She lay with him. Servants bound her children's arms
around the fading body's feebleness.
She lay on top of him for sweet long hours,
a little frightened of his many years.

And sometimes, when an owl was shrieking,
she turned her face away from his old beard
and everything the night contained came near
to her with fear and anxious longing.

Just like herself the stars were trembling,
the fragrance wafted searching through the room,
the curtain stirred itself and gave a sign
and silently she followed with her eyes.

But still she held onto the dark old man,
and not acceded by the night of nights
she lay down on his princely coldness there
a virgin and a weightless soul, so light.

Eve

(Rainer Maria Rilke)

She stands simply at the cathedral's great
staircase, near the rose window
holding the apple in that apple-pose
guiltless-guilty once for all times at

the growing being that she bore
since lovingly she left the circle
of eternities to battle through earth,
so much like a young year.

Oh, she would have liked to stay a while
longer in that country to understand
the animals' concord without guile.

But as she found the man determined
she went with him looking for death,
and yet she hardly knew her God.

Adam

after Rainer Maria Rilke

He stands amazed at the cathedral's
steep staircase, near to the rose window,
as if frightened by the apotheosis
which was growing and diminishing him

at one stroke above this one and that one.
And he stands tall and is pleased while it lasts,
simply determined like a ploughman
who began and knew not how to find

the exit from the fully-finished
garden Eden into the new earth.
God was hard to be persuaded.

Again and again he threatened him
he will die rather than be granted his way.
But the man insisted: she will give birth.

The King
(Rainer Maria Rilke)

The king is sixteen years of age.
Sixteen years and a state already.
As from an ambush he is looking away
past the ancient counsellors to see

into the chamber and anywhere else
and feels perhaps only just this:
by the narrow length of the hard chin,
the cold chain of the fleece.

The sentence of death in front of him
stays long without signature.
And they're thinking: how he tortures himself.

They would guess if they knew him well enough
that he's slowly counting to seventy
before he signs his name.

Esther

after Rainer Maria Rilke

For seven days the servant girls were combing
her sorrow's and low spirit's ashes
from her hair and took it out into
the sunshine in the open air and fed it
spices still today and several days: but then

the time had come when leaning on her servants,
without an invitation or appointment,
like someone dead, she went into the threatening
unlocked palace and saw him facing her
whose presence can cause death when coming near.

He shone so much, she felt the ruby flaming
out inside the coronet she wore;
she quickly filled herself with his whole air
just like a vessel that was full enough

and overflowed with power of the king,
before she'd walked across the third great hall
flooded by greenness of the malachite.
She had not thought to walk so long with all these stones
becoming heavier with the king's bright light
and cold with her own fear. She walked and walked.

And as she saw him near at last, resting
and towering on the throne of tourmaline,
so real and powerful, so like a thing:

she fainted in the servant woman's arms
who led her to the seat. He touched her
with his sceptre's point and she was without
senses, comprehending it, inside.

Palm
(Rainer Maria Rilke)

Inside of the hand., Sole that only walks on
feeling now, nothing more; opening up
to a mirror
conceiving heavenly streets, they too are
moving ones.
That has learnt to walk on the water
it gathers,
that walks on the well's rim,
transforming every road and lane.
That appears inside other hands
creating with them
the same landscape:
moving and arriving in them,
fullness of arrival.

A Fading
(Rainer Maria Rilke)

Lightly, as if after her death,
she carried the gloves, the shawl.
From her chest of drawers the air
is supplanting the kind smell

she used to know herself by.
Now she's not been asking for a while
who she might be (a distant relative)
and walks about thoughtfully

and cares for an anxious room
which she tidies and preserves
because the same girl
is still living here, perhaps.

It is a Castle
(Rainer Maria Rilke)

It is a castle. The fading
coat of arms above the gate.
Tree tops grow like fleeing
hands higher in front.

A gleaming blue flower
rose in the slowly sinking
window for show.

Not a weeping woman –
she is the last one waving
in the broken building.

From: Late Poems
Rainer Maria Rilke

Don't put your trust wholly in books, they are
the have-beens and the future times. Get hold
of being now. So your maturity won't be
complete when everyone is still a child.

There things are standing endlessly surpassing
that which is drawn together in our minds;
we only guess and everyone is questioned,
but they go inward and remain determined.

And even if you did begin your life
as if in hours you should overcome it:
you'll find a master in the smallest thing
and never can do justice to his inner kind.

Autumn
after Rainer Maria Rilke

The leaves are falling, falling as from far,
from distant gardens in the skies;
they fall with gestures that say 'no' to life.

And heavy earth is falling down at night
into the solitude from every star.

We are all falling. There, this hand will fall.
And look at others: all contain this fate.

And yet there's One whose constancy will hold
this falling in the mildest hands of all.

Winter Stanzas

after Rainer Maria Rilke

Now we should endure those bygone days
a long time in the rind of resistance, always
rejecting, never letting the cheek feel
the depth of rising winds.
The night is strong, yet the weak lamp
gently persuades the distant walking.
Be comforted: frost and harshness prepare
the tension of future acceptances.

Have you yet quite experienced the roses
of last summer? Feel, consider:
the restedness of pure morning hours,
the light walk in cobwebbed paths?
Plunge down inside yourself, shake, excite
the dear joy: it has vanished inside you.
And when you perceive one thing that escaped
be glad to start again from the very beginning.

Perhaps the radiance of doves, circling,
a tune of birds, almost like suspicion,
the gaze of flowers (mostly overlooked),
a fragrant expectation before night.
Nature is God complete. Who can compete
unless a God creates it naturally?
Because receiving it so inwardly
is holding it fulfilled in his own hands.

Is holding surfeit and abundance
without the hope of any other newness,
is holding surfeit and abundance
without surmising something was escaping,
is holding surfeit and abundance
with all his longing more than satisfied
and was astonished at this calm acceptance
of the unsteady mightiness of plenty.

Only
Richard Dehmel (1863-1920)

And this parting was no ending,
and my eyes could move you still:
and it was your heart that filled
silently my hands for tending.

But when you return at last,
I'll not touch your hand with kissing:
I will only sense and listen
how you fend against your heart.

Moon and Drinker
after Rudolf Binding

Go sleep, O Moon,
sleep tight on to my beaker.
I'm watching you.
I look at you, O Moon, a boozer
still as you.

So still as you
with you and nearly dying
I wander through a nightly territory.
We watch each other.
You're drinking from my beaker:
we are equality.

Mathilde Poems
after Heinrich Heine

Words! Words! No action ever!
Never meat, beloved Dolly,
Always intellect, no roast beef,
In the soup no dumplings for me!

But perhaps you are not partial
To the wild strength of the loins
That in gallop daily marshals
Horse and rider's fervent passions.

Yes, I fear almost, it causes
Near exhaustion, tender child,
This mad hunt of love that races
Cupid's steeple-chase of old.

So I say, far better for you,
Much more healthy, I would think,
Is a sick man as a lover
Who, like me, can't move his limbs.

Therefore dedicate your impulse
To our heart's close bond, my darling,
It will keep you strong and healthy
In a kind of wholesome loving.

All your youth ...
(Stefan George)

All your youth flowed like a dance,
A game intoxicated with horn and flute?
"Lord, I tempted thus your sons of light.
  For your song I forswore human happiness
  Submitted to the need of wandering
  Exploring them till I would find you there ...
  I did this every day and night
  Ever since remembering my life:
  Searching for you on path and stile."

I Live ...
(Magister Martinus, 1498)

I live and don't know how long,
I die and don't know when,
I move and don't know where to:
I'm wondering how happy I am.